IMAGINE A HEALTHY YOU

A Book Full of Powerful Secrets for Your Recovery.

A Step-by-Step Guide for Increased Wellness and Healing for Patients, Families, Friends, and Caregivers

Ulrike Berzau

and

Christel Cowdrey

BALBOA
PRESS
A DIVISION OF HAY HOU

D1414115

Balboa Press books may be ordered through booksellers or by contacting:

Balboa Press
A Division of Hay House
1663 Liberty Drive
Bloomington, IN 47403
www.balboapress.com
1 (877) 407-4847

Print information available on the last page.

ISBN: 978-1-4525-9892-5 (sc)
ISBN: 978-1-4525-9894-9 (hc)
ISBN: 978-1-4525-9893-2 (e)

Library of Congress Control Number: 2014920548

Balboa Press rev. date: 2/23/2015

Book cover by www.virtualgraphicartsdepartment.com

This book is dedicated to those of you who are
in the process of recovery and renewal.

Here we shall explore the power of the mind, how it
can heal the body, and how you can use your own power
to improve your physical and mental performance.

Enjoying this new focus, you will be able to complete
daily tasks and all your activities with greater ease.

This book has been written for *you*!

We want to show you how you may guide yourself
and, in turn, help your loved ones and those needing
support to press on to a life of improved wellbeing.

Practicing imagery provides an amazing opportunity for
anyone and everyone to promote recovery and healing.

FOREWORD BY BOB PROCTOR

I've been teaching people about the power of the mind for over 50 years now. And I've found that most people, once they *really* start listening to and processing the information I share, pretty readily accept the idea that their thoughts directly create their results ... up to a certain point.

Most can believe that their thoughts can transform their financial situation ... their relationships ... their career. They can be convinced that virtually everything in their lives is within their control to significantly impact and improve.

Then we get to health.

The fact is, many people believe that health limitations simply cannot be breached by the power of thought—even people who have acknowledged it as the most formidable force in the world. They view health as somehow separate; beyond the laws which they can see govern every other aspect of the universe.

Now that's a funny thing. Because the direct connection between the mind and the body might just be the MOST studied and established one of all. It has been explored and confirmed by some of the greatest philosophers, healers, and physicians of all time, going back thousands of years and continuing right up to this day.

Ulrike Berzau and Christel Cowdrey are two of the latest thinkers to take up this exploration. They have both experienced firsthand the incontrovertible power of the mind to help and heal the body. In their profoundly wise, sympathetic, and accessible book, they have brought something fresh and powerful to this esteemed area of study and inquiry.

If you are suffering from chronic pain, fatigue, illness, or any other physical malady that restricts your mobility, activity, peace of mind, or enjoyment of life—or are close to someone who is—these pages will pave a path of relief for you. And, even if your challenges have not manifested in physical symptoms, there is so much benefit to be mined from the personal stories and practical exercises Ulrike and Christel share.

The question isn't *can* the mind help to heal the body. That has been answered beyond the shadow of the doubt by countless people, many of whom you'll read about in this book. The question is, when will YOU begin to direct your extraordinary thought-power toward the critical end of creating and maintaining vibrant health and wellbeing.

Start today. With Ulrike and Christel as your learned and caring guides, you will be infinitely richer, better, and healthier for it—inside and out.

Bob Proctor
Best-selling author of You Were Born Rich

PREFACE

From Me to You

A Message from Ulrike

After working for many years in
health care as a physical therapist
and health care executive, I have
witnessed many peoples' life-
changing events, illnesses, and
recoveries.

Photo by Diane Maehl

I have seen how powerful the human mind is and how much
our mindset affects our mind, our body, our soul, and, most
importantly, our results.

I have often wondered why people feel fatigued, have chronic
pain, or get sick for no obvious reason, especially when
traditional medicine can find no cause. I have also seen amazing

recoveries from illness and injuries when physicians and health care providers expected little or no recovery.

For many years, I have been intrigued by the holistic approach to healing and have learned, followed, and experimented with complementary, integrative medicine approaches. There is tremendous value in integrative medicine and treatments that complement the traditional medicine approach.

But it was not until I learned about the power of our mind that I understood fully how everything affects our health, wellbeing, and recovery.

I have had the opportunity to study with the world's experts in this field, and I am delighted to be able to share with you how your mind can transform your health and wellbeing.

It is so simple and it is so powerful.

We all have this ability; we just have to learn how to flex our mental muscles.

From Me to You

A Message from Christel

My Swedish upbringing was founded in health. Finding peace in our pursuits and having fun were highlighted every day. We were not permitted to indulge in boredom.

I believe this was the case because we needed encouragement through the long winters of Scandinavia, where it is pitch-black for months. We were encouraged to be in charge of our thoughts.

Like most children, I was good at the things I loved. I understood pretty quickly that my focus and thoughts created either a good result or a bad one. I have always submitted to the power of a greater sovereignty than the tiny atom that is me.

I have always understood that the mind is a powerhouse. I have watched and observed people I think of as successful, noticing that their power lies in their belief in themselves; they trust themselves and their goal or focus. The bigger their need to succeed, the faster the success and the finishing of that task, before they soared up into the next dream or desire impatiently waiting in line, tapping its foot.

I had been visualizing long before I understood its effects. I researched it, studied it, worked with it, and accelerated my understanding of it for many years, so I find the information in this book exhilarating and in line with the mostly untapped powerhouse of our minds.

The exercises in chapter 14 are so simple; they just require a little practice for you to sink into the peace of your imagination, the wondrous place where all harmony and wellness lies.

We are blessed, of course, with the scientific research that launches this book into the world with the wind at its back. I hope you find our excitement contagious.

I wish you the success that is inevitable on the journey you are about to take. Do so at your own pace. I wish you the same thrill I feel when I submit to the journey of my mind.

CHAPTER 1

VISUALIZATION

You may be familiar with visualization, the gentle step towards the imagined events or objects in your mind's eye, helping you to achieve your desired outcome. Everybody has the ability to visualize, and we use this ability all the time—but not always to achieve the results we seek.

Visualization is as simple as imagining the color of your car when someone asks you about it. When you think about the car's color, you immediately bring your car to mind, thereby identifying its color.

Visualization techniques are strengthened and become imagery when you impress your feelings and your senses upon the picture in your mind. You make the images brighter and stronger by adding color, sound, smell, taste, and touch. In this way you are creating your own movie and can play it over and over in your mind.

"Logic will get you from A-Z; imagination will get you everywhere."

— Albert Einstein

CHAPTER 2

HOW CELEBRITIES AND OLYMPIC MEDALISTS USE IMAGERY

Many athletes and celebrities have discovered the miraculous power of visualization and imagery and have used it to enhance their careers and performance.

Oprah Winfrey frequently mentions the power of the subconscious mind, the importance of focusing on goals, and the effectiveness of visualization techniques. She uses vision boards to enhance her visualizations. Oprah is quoted as saying, "The biggest adventure you can take is to live the life of your dreams." So visualization and imagery put the life in your dreams.

The highly accomplished golfer Tiger Woods started using visualization at a very early age. He has extensively used the astounding power of his mind to create pictures and to imagine exactly where he wants his golf ball to go and to stop. He has envisaged and enhanced his mission and his win, time and time again.

Before becoming governor of California, Arnold Schwarzenegger used visualization techniques to accomplish his dreams as a bodybuilder from a young age. In his imagination, he became Mr. Universe, acting as if he had already taken the title. Arnold Schwarzenegger did indeed become Mr. Universe.

Visualization has long been a part of the elite sports, but recently the practice of mental and motor imagery has advanced significantly. Sports psychologists stress that the more athletes can imagine their performance and the outcome, the better their performance will be.

For example, imagery was consistently applied during the Sochi Olympics. Olympians were seen preparing themselves using imagery, and once they received their medals, they shared that they had visualized reaching their goals for many years. They would say such things as, "I imagined each part of the run and saw myself standing here. I always dreamed of receiving this medal."

A February 22, 2014, in the *New York Times,* says that Emily Cook, a member of the United States freestyle ski team competing in Sochi, visualized each aerial jump as part of her training for the Olympics. She shared her visualization, identifying the most important parts she applied to her training: "For me, visualization takes in all the senses. I have to smell it, hear it, feel it, imagine, everything."

Emily had become an expert in including imagery in her daily competition routine. She simulated jumps with robotic precision and absorbed the imagined impact of the landings. When she finished a session that required only about two minutes to complete, she was flushed with the effort.

The *New York Times* article further states that Olympic Canadian bobsledder Lyndon Rush said that, before competing, he mentally drove the Sochi course hundreds of times, from start to finish. "I've tried to keep the track in my mind throughout the year," he said. "I would be in the shower or brushing my teeth. It just takes a minute, so I do the whole thing or sometimes just the corners that are more technical; I must keep it fresh in my head, so when I get there, I am not starting at square one. It's amazing how much you can do with your mind."

Mikaela Shiffrin, the then-eighteen-year-old American skier, said that she had already mentally simulated many aspects of her first trip to the Olympics and therefore didn't feel like an amateur, she certainly did not ski like an amateur. She won the slalom.

As Emily shared so well, effective imagery is a multisensory experience. We move beyond visualization to imagery by using our five senses to create a mental picture and, more importantly, the feeling associated with our desired outcome.

Many athletes create scripts, writing down their practice in detail and adding many audio and sensory experiences. During their training and before their completion, the athletes regularly listen to the recording and go through their actual performance step-by-step. So it is clear that athletes can enhance their performance through visualization and imagery.

It is a well-known fact that, once injured, athletes also use imagery to speed up the healing process, and some report they can even feel their bones heal. Research has confirmed the effectiveness of the power of imagery in healing and recovery. Our minds truly determine our outcomes, and it is a privilege to share with you here how the power of our minds affects not only our performance but also our wellbeing and recovery.

In this book, we will explore how the power of your mind affects your body and wellbeing. We will explore the importance of our self-image, what shapes and influences it, and with this new found knowledge, how we can use the power of our mind to improve our ability to function and to perform movements, activities, and sports.

> "The knowledge and the power to alter the course of your health are within you!"
>
> —Bob Proctor, *The Cure Is ...*

"The mind is the greatest power in all of creation."

~ Dr. J.B. Rhine

"The world as we have created it is a process of our thinking. It cannot be changed without changing our thinking."

— Albert Einstein

CHAPTER 3

OUR PARADIGMS AND THE AUTOPILOT THAT DRIVES OUR LIVES

Have you ever thought about the image you have of yourself—your self-image? Have you done certain things because you believed you could? The image we have of ourselves has a miraculous effect on our results and truly determines those results.

Each of us carries within us an emotional and mental blueprint of our self-image, and our feelings and behaviors are consistent with this inner picture. Our self-image is the picture of the person we think we are, and it is shaped early in our childhood.

Most of us vividly remember what our parents and teachers told us; we remember experiences with our teachers, friends, and others who influenced us. Past experiences are the sculpting factors of a strong, successful self-image or the opposite: limiting beliefs.

What is imprinted in your subconscious mind is the result of other people's input, your past successes and disappointments, your achievements, and your embarrassments.

We all are susceptible to the input of others and the experiences we had as children, but we are continually being reshaped. When our life is affected by disease or injury, our self-image is also affected. The good news is that you can regain functions, renew your body, and change how you feel by changing the image you have of yourself.

> "Our success in any undertaking will never be greater than the image we have of ourselves."
>
> —Bob Proctor

CHAPTER 4

THE CONSCIOUS AND SUBCONSCIOUS MIND

Before going deeper into the subject of self-image, let's explore how our mind works.

Our mind is a function, not just an anatomical brain. We have a conscious mind and a subconscious mind. The subconscious determines our body's actions and the results. The conscious mind allows us to accept and reject thoughts and experiences. We receive input through our five senses: vision, hearing, smell, taste, and touch. Our senses run endlessly and readily absorb information from the "outside"—for example, from the radio, TV, Internet, and other people.

Once our conscious mind accepts the input, especially if a thought is coupled with repetition and emotion, it is absorbed into our subconscious. The subconscious mind accumulates input and becomes the warehouse of our deep-seated beliefs, our habits, our self-image, and simply said our paradigm.

As you read this today, you have the ability to accept or reject what you are reading; you can simply filter any input that your five senses are intuitively picking up.

The Mind of an Infant

The conscious mind of an infant is not developed enough to filter impressions; therefore, environmental input is immediately absorbed by the infant's subconscious mind. Herein lies the development of the paradigm.

Interestingly, infants already hear and recognize their mother's and other people's voices in the womb and pick up on emotions. If the mother is worried, or relaxed and confident, this transfers straight into the infant's subconscious and shapes his or her paradigm.

So, why is the experience we store in our subconscious mind so important? Simply, our subconscious mind is our feeling and emotional mind and determines our body's actions and therefore our results. Our outer world is a reflection of our paradigm imprinted in our subconscious mind.

"Whatever we plant in our subconscious mind and nourish with repetition and emotion will one day become a reality."

—Earl Nightingale

CHAPTER 5

PHYSICIANS' RESPECT FOR THE POWER OF IMAGERY

Let us now explore how our paradigm, which includes our self-image, affects our actions and results. Dr. Maxwell Maltz, a renowned plastic surgeon, began to study the outcomes of his patients after he was surprised with their post-surgical results. His findings were published in the book *Psycho-Cybernetics* in 1960.

While studying the outcomes and psychological changes of his patients after plastic surgery, Dr. Maltz came to the conclusion that we actually have two images: one is the image that we see in the mirror and the other is the image of ourselves that we hold in our mind.

With that knowledge, Dr. Maltz was intrigued by the power of the self-image and the "autopilot" that drives our lives. He pointed out that the result of this paradigm, which includes the self-image, is due to a cybernetic mechanism.

Cybernetics is a self-regulating control mechanism—a system of control and emergent behavior. For example, the temperature control in a building is a cybernetic mechanism. Another example is an airplane's autopilot that flies a plane from one city or country to its destination.

Today we build on the knowledge of self-image and cybernetic principles to help people understand how their self-image has control over their ability to achieve, or failure to achieve, a goal. The self-image is the set destination, and our actions and behaviors continuously adjust to make sure we reach that set destination. Understanding psycho-cybernetics principles allows you to awaken your automatic success mechanism and frees you from beliefs that hold you back.

"You can always tell what's happening on the inside by what's happening on the outside."

—Bob Proctor

CHAPTER 6

THE POWER OF YOUR MIND, AND BRINGING IT ALL TOGETHER

The power of mental pictures and an understanding of psycho-cybernetics open the door to improved performance for professional athletes as well as improved function for patients in rehabilitation.

Motor imagery is the mind imagining an action or function of the body without performing it; this is an important element in self-healing and is increasingly practiced. Visualization stimulates your mind and body and creates an automatic mechanism for healing and recovery. Imagination triggers your body's autonomic physiological responses, which, if constructive, support the healing process. We can improve motor function, resulting in a better rehabilitative outcome, by exercising the knowledge of imagery and the automatic success mechanism.

We know the body's performance is an expression and an extension of what is going on in our mind. The subconscious doesn't know the difference between what is "real" and what is imagined; it doesn't discern or consider a difference between an outer experience and an inner experience.

The results of imagery are amplified through tapping into emotions and with repetition.

Mental pictures and motor imagery are mighty concepts, and the results are stunning!

" If we are creating ourselves all the time, then it is never too late to begin creating the bodies we want instead of the ones we mistakenly assume we are stuck with."

— Deepak Chopra

"Imagination is more important than knowledge. For knowledge is limited to all we now know and understand, while imagination embraces the entire world, and all there ever will be to know and understand."

— Albert Einstein

CHAPTER 7

THE MASTERY OF IMAGERY

Once we begin to understand how the mind works and the results we are getting, we can use our mind to create an image of winning. Because our self-image leads us like an autopilot, many athletes develop and use their self-image to achieve astounding success. It's a powerful concept!

As we learned earlier, many Olympians speak of this process once they had received their medal:

"I visualized myself receiving this medal for many years."

"I visualized myself standing here."

"I knew I would get the medal."

"I always dreamed of receiving this medal."

Various studies have been conducted to measure the impact of the power of the mind, the power of our physical body, and the power of our activities. Your thoughts are vital, they really do affect your reality, positively or negatively, you decide.

In many published studies observing the effects of our mental focus on muscles and performance, one set of participants was asked to perform physical activities, and a second group was asked to visualize the same activity without performing it, complemented by visualization. Both groups saw an increase in muscle strength and performance.

Other studies asked participants to use motor imagery combined with or without physical training, and the results were compared to traditional physical performance training. The results proved that the athletes who practiced imagery showed the most improvement and enhanced performance.

What Does This Mean?

Your mind controls your body and your physical abilities as a whole. You need to understand that what exists in the world of your mind will also exist in your physical world. We all think in images; once coupled with repetition and emotion, these images become our world.

The many stories of athletes achieving amazing results through goal-directed motor imagery are promising. Imagine what you will experience with your individual goals when you put your creative mental muscles into action in your life.

Clear goals combined with a winning self-image allow you to taste success. Imagery is a very powerful, respected, and recognized concept.

CHAPTER 8

Take Charge of Your Destiny and Follow Your Dreams

It is really quite simple: if we can picture our success, it is likely that we will reach our goals and dreams.

> "Make the development of your healthy self-image your primary goal. See yourself as competent and deserving. Imagine yourself as confident and able to succeed in whatever project you undertake."
>
> —Jane Savoie

Jane Savoie is one of the most recognized names in United States dressage (an equestrian sport). She has a long list of accomplishments, including being a member of the United States Equestrian Team and an Olympic dressage coach.

Jane Savoie shares in her book *That Winning Feeling! A New Approach To Riding Using Psychocybernetics* more about the goal-striving mechanism that is embedded in our subconscious mind. Whatever clear goal we put in front of our subconscious mind, it will pursue. We can decide if we want to program our subconscious as a WIN or a LOSE mechanism. Jane Savoie describes the WIN mechanism, "I can Achieve **W**hatever **I** **N**eed and **WIN**," as an excellent example of mental function that produces positive benefits. This absolute focus and determination repeated in your thoughts, reprograms your subconscious mind.

The goal our mind pursues is the mental picture we create when we use our imagination. This is the picture we need to see and drop into our subconscious mind. It is irrelevant that the goal may seem out of reach or that you do not know how to achieve the desired end result. Just imagine your goal, see it and feel it, as though it is already in existence.

"Winners are dreamers who understand how to turn their dreams into reality and, in doing so, they create a better, more beautiful world for everyone."

—Bob Proctor

CHAPTER 9

MOTOR IMAGERY AND HEALING

Let's explore how we can apply this intriguing knowledge to anyone with physical and functional limitations, such as those who are suffering pain or fatigue or cognitive challenges.

A large volume of research has been conducted with patients suffering neurological challenges and motor-skill limitations. A number of rehabilitation professionals use imagery in rehabilitation programs to support the relearning of motor ability. For increased movement, patients are taught to imagine, with repetition, specific desired physical actions as if they were actually performing those actions. For example, a patient recovering from a stroke focuses on raising his hand and his arm to bring a cup to his lips.

As noted, when athletes apply motor imagery alongside physical training, it has proved to be more effective than motor imagery or physical training alone. This knowledge can be transferred to physical rehabilitation and opens doors to improve the function of people in any physical rehabilitation program. Research has shown that, during motor imagery sessions, the same brain areas are activated as during functional tasks; therefore, the same changes in the motor system may occur as the result of actual movements.

Our actions are the result of the image we plant in our mind.

A Powerful Tool for Us All: The Freedom to Create Using the Power of Our Imagination

Any one of us can practice imagery at any time, on our own. For example, while resting or after physical activities, you can practice using your mind to rehearse the desired movements and results.

When you practice motor imagery, it does not matter if your body is able to complete the physical task fully, partially, or even at all. The mental picture combined with the feeling of excitement, and the thought of being able to perform the movement and its repetition, is the key to your success.

We know now that, through imagery, the success mechanism for functional and cognitive recovery is set in motion. The power of motor imagery complements the healing process and allows a more holistic approach to rehabilitation and recovery. The results are astounding!

"The way you think, the way you behave, the way you eat, can influence your life by 30 to 50 years."

— Deepak Chopra

CHAPTER 10

THE RELENTLESS AND ABUNDANT POWER OF THE MIND

The following exercise can help you use the power of the mind to heal your body.

The First Step

Allow yourself to forget the past and put your limitations aside for now. Start to plant the desired image of the "ultimate you" in your subconscious mind.

Ask yourself,

- How has the image of myself changed through my illness or injury?

- What is the image I am holding of myself?
- What is the image of my most empowered self?

You and Your Awareness

Examine your mind and body: What are you thinking and feeling? What is it that you believe about your health? Why do you believe this?

Question your thoughts and beliefs; be brave and turn them around. Create a positive image for each negative one.

Say Hello to Your Faith

Believe and expect that you are *already* well. In this moment; believe and expect that you have perfect health. See yourself in perfect health and able to move as you desire. *This is your task: you must believe and must expect a healthy you.*

With the knowledge of how your mind works and with an understanding of the power of your subconscious mind and how it affects your body, you are off to a great start. The next step is to believe and expect health and wellbeing.

Having faith means to believe in the unseen. Even the Bible notes, "Now faith is the substance of things hoped for, the evidence of things not seen" (Hebrews 11:1, King James Version).

Your Renewal

"You can rewrite your life; you can rewrite your health at any time you choose to; your body was created to do this; it is happening every day."

—Bob Proctor, *The Cure Is …*

"Our body creates new cells and our whole life is recreated every few months."

—Deepak Chopra

We have a built-in system to keep our body in fine order. The body heals itself without assistance. When you cut your skin, for example, it spontaneously initiates a healing response.

> "When we change the way we think, we change our lives; what most people do not understand is how powerful our thinking is and how involved it is in our health crisis."
>
> —Bob Proctor, *The Cure Is …*

CHAPTER 11

LIVING YOUR GOAL IN EVERY MOMENT OF YOUR DAY

Before we explore actual imagery, let us review the power of the goal. Athletes and many peak-performing individuals use the power of goal setting, which is essential to effectively using visualization and imagery.

If you are in a rehabilitation process, goals are determined after a thorough assessment by a rehabilitation team. It is important to work with the physical, occupational, or speech therapists and anyone else on a rehabilitation team on these goals and action steps.

It is imperative to trust your own sense of healing, too. What is your big goal, your true desire, your dream?

Your True Desire: The Mastery of Your Magnificent Mind

Your big dream is what we want to explore here. A true desire is a big goal, a dream that excites and scares us at the same time.

After injury or illness, your functional and cognitive independence and the ability to do activities may be impaired or painful.

Consider what you would like to be able to do again with ease?

Your true desire is the highest level of your goal, and we encourage you to pursue that. What excites you? Let your imagination flow. Again, know that you will feel a bit apprehensive, perhaps frightened, when you think about your big goal. If you do not, your goal is not big enough. Once you are clear on your big goal, you can use imagery to pursue it.

When imagining your goal, it is important to "start with the end in mind," according to Stephen Covey. That means focusing on the final, desired outcome. For example, instead of focusing on raising the weak or paralyzed arm, think about an activity you wish to complete. When needing to re-learn how to walk, think about walking with ease in your house, your garden or your favorite trail, rather than working on leg strength and movement alone.

After an injury or if you are suffering a disease, don't give up! Now you have the opportunity to put your imagination and mind to work. Search for your goal, your biggest desire.

There are two methods you can explore to pursue your desired results.

1. *One gentle step at a time.* Focus on the process, one gentle step at a time. In the sports analogy described earlier, athletes think about each step of the movement, the game, the activity—one step at a time. When you focus on the process, you imagine the actual movement you desire—for example, raising your arm to taste your

favorite drink or food, walking step-by-step with ease, or climbing the stairs one step at a time.

2. *The outcome is the prize.* Focus on the outcome, the prize, or the medal. In the sports analogy, athletes imagine achieving their win and receiving their medal at an awards ceremony. Here they are imagining the outcome, the prize they are going to achieve. You too can see the outcome: eating your favorite food after bringing it to your mouth, seeing your family applaud you after you walk a long distance, or spending time with your family in the garden because you were able to walk there alone.

Begin with the end in mind.

CHAPTER 12

USE THE POWER OF YOUR MIND; IT'S ALL YOURS

"The imagination is the mental faculty out of
which visions arise."

—Sandy Gallagher

Step 1: Understanding Yourself.
Where Do You Find Yourself?

Understanding where you are is an important first step.
Explore your self-image. How did your self-image change
due to your illness or injury? What do you believe you can do
right now?

Once you understand your self-image and are aware of any limiting beliefs, you will understand your mental condition. Again, the paradigm that includes your self-image is your autopilot, so it is always in the driver's seat.

Step 2: Define Your Goal

The next step is to turn your self-image upside down and replace it with the picture of the person you truly desire to be as well as the movements and activities you want to experience. In this step, allow yourself to define your goals—the really big goals, and the picture of your dreams. Do not worry about how you'll get there; use your imagination to paint the picture and imprint it on your mind.

Step 3: Plant the Image of Your Biggest Goal In Your Mind

We all have an abundance of creative faculties; imagination is but one, and it is necessary to create your desired outcome.

The sky is the limit!

Do not settle for what you *think* you can achieve, but go for what you really *want*! Dream big and bold. Have fun with it!

Once you have formed the picture of what you want in your mind, add your feelings and your emotion to it. Include the quality of the movements you want to experience, such as strength, endurance, ease, and freedom from discomfort or pain. Live the finest image of yourself in your imagination.

It is important to add feeling to your image and to engage your five senses, always holding the image and living it over and over until it is embedded deeply in your subconscious mind.

Release Worry, Visualization Is the Path To Success

"Everyone visualizes, whether they know it or not. Visualizing is the great secret to success."

— Genevieve Behrend

It is noteworthy that most of us worry and visualize everything we do not want to have or be, not quite understanding that the more emotion we lavishly pour over our fear, the more likely it will become reality. Too often, we relive negative experiences and disappointments, focusing on these instead of using our imagination to create a great future for ourselves.

CHAPTER 13

WAVING THE MAGIC WAND AND CHANGING THE OUTCOME

Changing your thinking from the things you don't want or you can't change to positive thoughts can bring quite magical results.

Find and create the space and time to focus on your true desires, your big goals, your dreams. Write your goals down. Writing creates the image and the image creates the feeling. Putting your thoughts into words powerfully drops the picture into your subconscious mind.

When you start using imagery, you will become more aware of your thoughts and notice that most of your thinking revolves around the things that are difficult or situations that worry you. Many of our thoughts during the day are about the past, or worry for the future. Place such thoughts aside. Cast them away. They have no place in your world. *Change comes only when you focus on what you truly want!*

Remember that your subconscious doesn't distinguish between what is real and what is imagined. Remember the lemon example when you get discouraged; remember how strongly your body reacts to the pure imagination of a lemon.

Enjoy using your imagination to achieve your desired outcome. Your self-image, once in step with your imagination, will be in the driver's seat and keep you on course to your goal.

CHAPTER 14

DAILY EXERCISES TO DEVELOP THE DESIRED YOU

To ignite your ability to imagine a healthy you, the following exercises recall activities that you used to enjoy. Each one begins with a prelude, starting with this:

Find a comfortable place where you are undisturbed.

Depending on your mobility, sit or lie down.

Take a deep breath and hold it for four

seconds. Slowly exhale for seven.

Repeat this three times. Enjoy your calm breathing.

Then remembering the physical activities or sport you enjoyed in the past, you will playfully experience all the ways you used your hands, arms, legs, and your body with ease.

Enjoy the memories of how easy it felt. Explore some specific movements and activities that were familiar to you. Imagine performing your favorite activities.

Go into more detail with one of your favorite activities. How did it feel when you used to enjoy this activity?

Add as much detail as possible to the activity by using your five senses. What do you see, hear, smell, taste, and touch?

In the following imagery practices, you will use the power of imagination coupled with your five senses and emotions. This is where the magic is!

With your imagination, you will be adding new skills to your memory—skills you will master. These exercises focus specifically on daily activities that you need to do to embrace your independence, including specific activities to improve the function of any weakened part of your body.

According to your ease of movement and your comfort, choose the activities you wish to improve. For optimized benefit, read and practice the breathing and the relaxation exercises before you begin any of the exercises that follow.

THE SHOWER

Find a comfortable place where you are undisturbed.

Depending on your mobility, sit or lie down. Take a deep

breath and hold it for four seconds. Slowly exhale for seven.

Repeat this three times. Enjoy your calm breathing.

Imagine that a cleansing light enters your

body from the crown of your head.

This vibrant light flows through your body, drawing

away all worries, all pain, all tears, all fears—

sweeping healing comfort and fresh energy into your

body. You feel at peace, supported, not alone.

Imagine this abundant healing light coming in and flowing

through to the tips of your fingers, to the tips of your toes,

cleansing and revitalizing every precious part of you.

The light leaves your body, drawing with it all

impurities, leaving you free of disease and anything

that may hinder your happiness and your health.

Imagine taking a shower, seeing the steam on the shower door and hearing the water splashing.

The shower gel smells refreshing.

You may get a drop of water in your mouth; it tastes refreshing. Take your time to feel the water touching your skin; enjoy this wonderful long shower. How does the shower gel feel on your skin? Perhaps you enjoy using a sponge to scrub and massage your skin gently.

Add a little bit of luxury by imagining a scent used in aromatherapy; it could be vanilla, lavender, lemon, or any of your favorite scents.

Relish each moment in your wonderful shower imagination. Stepping out of your shower, towel off your body. How does it feel?

Take your time to enjoy the feeling. Do you remember your body lotion? Apply it to your skin and enjoy the feeling of the lotion and the touch of your skin. What is the perfume of your lotion? Imagine an aroma of your liking.

During this and all the exercises, stay in the moment. It is not important that you remember everything from the past; it is important to engage your five senses and your feelings. Get emotionally involved to develop the desired you. The more you can fully engage in these experiences, the stronger the effect on your body.

Try to embellish each "picture." For example, if you love taking a shower, include all the luxurious elements that spring to mind. If this example does not engage you, choose a different activity. The key is to live the activity as though it were real, to truly enjoy it with all your feelings and emotions.

ENCOURAGING ARM AND HAND MOVEMENTS: DRINKING A CAPPUCCINO

Find a comfortable place where you are undisturbed.

Depending on your mobility, sit or lie down. Take a deep

breath and hold it for four seconds. Slowly exhale for seven.

Repeat this three times. Enjoy your calm breathing.

Imagine that a cleansing light enters your

body from the crown of your head.

This vibrant light flows through your body, drawing

away all worries, all pain, all tears, all fears—

sweeping healing comfort and fresh energy into your

body. You feel at peace, supported, not alone.

Imagine this abundant healing light coming in and

flowing through to the tips of your fingers, to the tips

of your toes, cleansing and revitalizing every precious

part of you. The light leaves your body, drawing with it

all impurities, leaving you free of disease and anything

that may hinder your happiness and your healing.

Focus on a time when you were eating
and drinking independently.
Imagine sitting at your kitchen or dinner table,
or in your favorite coffee shop or restaurant.
Start with your favorite drink—for example, a cappuccino (in
the following, substitute the cappuccino with your favorite).
Imagine a mouthwatering, creamy, delicious cappuccino.
The froth on the top has a heart design
made with chocolate sprinkles.
You enjoy how artistically it has been prepared.
Put the little spoon in the saucer, and stir the froth a little.
How does the spoon feel? Is it silver or
plastic, smooth or textured?
Maybe you like to taste the froth and the
chocolate sprinkles on the top.
How enjoyable this is!
Now, as you place the spoon to the side of the cup, it
touches the cup or mug. Is it porcelain, or a textured
mug, or just a paper cup? How does it feel?
Is it warm? Enjoy the feeling of it.

Take the cup and bring it to your mouth to drink.

The anticipation of tasting it, what a pleasure it is!

Enjoy the moment before tasting the drink.

Feel the froth of the cappuccino on your lips.

Taste the rich creaminess of the coffee.

Quite delicious!

Repeat the imagery until you have finished

the drink in your imagination.

What a joy this is!

Encouraging Arm and Hand Movements: Enjoying Your Favorite Food

. . . .

Find a comfortable place where you are undisturbed.

Depending on your mobility, sit or lie down. Take a deep

breath and hold it for four seconds. Slowly exhale for seven.

Repeat this three times. Enjoy your calm breathing.

Imagine that a cleansing light enters your

body from the crown of your head.

This vibrant light flows through your body, drawing

away all worries, all pain, all tears, all fears—

sweeping healing comfort and fresh energy into your

body. You feel at peace, supported, not alone.

Imagine this abundant healing light coming in and flowing

through to the tips of your fingers, to the tips of your toes,

cleansing and revitalizing every precious part of you.

The light leaves your body, drawing with it all

impurities, leaving you free of disease and anything

that may hinder your happiness and your healing.

Focus on a moment when you were eating your favorite food.

Imagine sitting in your kitchen, or at your dinner table, or in a coffee shop or restaurant.

Start with something delicious that you enjoy, such as homemade bread.

(Substitute the bread with one of your favorite foods.)

Imagine a delicious and freshly baked loaf of bread, slightly doughy on the inside, with a dark crust on the outside.

You see the texture; it is made with whole grains, and the outside is golden.

You break off a piece. How do you find the texture? Is it still warm? Warm bread can be mouthwatering.

Isn't the anticipation of tasting it amazing? In your imagination, take the piece of bread and bring it to your mouth. We enjoy the moment immensely before we taste something.

Then, when we bite into it, it's crusty, making crunchy sounds.

Feeling the bread between your teeth, enjoy the moment. Take your time, chewing it piece by piece.

Repeat this in your imagination.

Absolutely delicious!

THE SIMPLE JOY OF WALKING

Find a comfortable place where you are undisturbed.

Depending on your mobility, sit or lie down. Take a deep

breath and hold it for four seconds. Slowly exhale for seven.

Repeat this three times. Enjoy your calm breathing.

Imagine that a cleansing light enters your

body from the crown of your head.

This vibrant light flows through your body, drawing

away all worries, all pain, all tears, all fears—

sweeping healing comfort and fresh energy into your

body. You feel at peace, supported, not alone.

Imagine this abundant healing light coming in and flowing

through to the tips of your fingers, to the tips of your toes,

cleansing and revitalizing every precious part of you.

The light leaves your body, drawing with it all

impurities, leaving you free of disease and anything

that may hinder your happiness and your healing.

Take steps and remember the simple joy of
walking. Your body moves with ease, and
you are walking in your favorite place.
Maybe you are in your garden, on your favorite trail, or
just walking through your neighborhood. Look around
you. What do you see? Flowers, birds in the trees,
foot paths, streams of water, a bridge over a river?
If you are walking through the woods, hear
and feel the breaking of twigs underfoot.
Perhaps it rained earlier and the ground is springy and soft.
Are there birds singing?
If you are close to a stream or river,
listen to the sound of the water.
Smell the fresh air, the flowers.
Taste the raindrops suspended in the
air, falling from the leaves.
Reach into the water and scoop it up.
Let it run through your fingers.
Taste berries. Touch the grass. Listen to
the breeze through the trees.
Continue walking, delighting in your five senses.
Enjoy the wonders of nature!

ESCAPING WITH EASE
INTO YOUR GARDEN

Find a comfortable place where you are undisturbed.

Depending on your mobility, sit or lie down. Take a deep

breath and hold it for four seconds. Slowly exhale for seven.

Repeat this three times. Enjoy your calm breathing.

Imagine that a cleansing light enters your

body from the crown of your head.

This vibrant light flows through your body, drawing

away all worries, all pain, all tears, all fears—

sweeping healing comfort and fresh energy into your

body. You feel at peace, supported, not alone.

Imagine this abundant healing light coming in and flowing

through to the tips of your fingers, to the tips of your toes,

cleansing and revitalizing every precious part of you.

The light leaves your body, drawing with it all

impurities, leaving you free of disease and anything

that may hinder your happiness and your healing.

As you stand in the wonderful garden you have always dreamed of, you are met by the humming of bees and the busy-ness of butterflies.

As you take off your shoes and walk on the newly mown grass, the aroma of the freshly cut lawn hits your senses. Breathe in deeply.

The flowers are in full bloom. There are red roses, white hydrangea, scented lilac bushes, lavender and jasmine climbing by the windows—nature set free. You are feeling the blessing of standing in this beauty and the clarity of the sunlight as it hits the flowers. You have bare feet on the grass, bare feet on God's earth. What a joyful experience on this vibrant day—the perfect temperature with the mildest of breezes on your face.

The herbs you have been tending are bushy and full, proud in their pots.

Meander silently through your garden, you are held there, still for a moment, listening to the birdsong. You are an onlooker with all the time in this world, and that nourishes your senses.

The light breeze blows your hair from

your face and caresses your skin.

The blackberries are ripe, you pick and taste a few,

knowing that the birds have eaten most. The berries burst

between your teeth, the sweetness lingers in your mouth.

You understand why people say there is God in every garden.

And so, with a deep and easy sigh, you

gently sink into your chair to rest.

BAKING A PIE

· ·

Find a comfortable place where you are undisturbed.

Depending on your mobility, sit or lie down. Take a deep

breath and hold it for four seconds. Slowly exhale for seven.

Repeat this three times. Enjoy your calm breathing.

Imagine that a cleansing light enters your

body from the crown of your head.

This vibrant light flows through your body, drawing

away all worries, all pain, all tears, all fears—

sweeping healing comfort and fresh energy into your

body. You feel at peace, supported, not alone.

Imagine this abundant healing light coming in and flowing

through to the tips of your fingers, to the tips of your toes,

cleansing and revitalizing every precious part of you.

The light leaves your body, drawing with it all

impurities, leaving you free of disease and anything

that may hinder your happiness and your healing.

Imagine you are preparing to bake your favorite pie. You are looking at the beautiful pies pictured in a cookbook. Which one would you like to bake: an apple, cherry, or apricot pie?

You can already hear your family and friends complimenting you on the delicious pie. They always say, "You make the most delicious pie in the world!"

Feel the flour on your hands, the dough pressed between your fingers. Add flour to keep it from sticking to your hands.

The dough is cool as you move it from one hand to the other and then put it on the floured work surface. Pressing down on the dough with your fingers and palms, you mold it into a circle ready for rolling.

The rolling pin is cold against the dough. You are rolling out the dough, feeling the pressure on your hands. You keep rolling.

Once the dough is ready, imagine as you carefully move it into the pan. Perhaps you fold it into quarters before placing it there; perhaps you just move it over.

You carefully press the dough into the pan and cut the edges that hang over with your knife. You pinch the crust between your forefinger and thumb. Then you add the fruit.

You enjoy the alluring aroma as your pie bakes, and you wait for it to be ready.

You long to take a piece, and whether you start with the crust or the fruit, you are enjoying every mouthful.

MOVING WITH EASE

Find a comfortable place where you are undisturbed.

Depending on your mobility, sit or lie down. Take a deep

breath and hold it for four seconds. Slowly exhale for seven.

Repeat this three times. Enjoy your calm breathing.

Imagine that a cleansing light enters your

body from the crown of your head.

This vibrant light flows through your body, drawing

away all worries, all pain, all tears, all fears—

sweeping healing comfort and fresh energy into your

body. You feel at peace, supported, not alone.

Imagine this abundant healing light coming in and flowing

through to the tips of your fingers, to the tips of your toes,

cleansing and revitalizing every precious part of you.

The light leaves your body, drawing with it all

impurities, leaving you free of disease and anything

that may hinder your happiness and your healing.

Imagine you are comfortably sitting in your favorite
chair and looking out the window. Outside,
there is sunshine and children are playing.
You decide to get up, and you slowly walk to the kitchen.
While you are walking, you breathe deeply
and enjoy how easily you seem to move.
You look around in the kitchen and hear music coming
from another room. It is your favorite music.
Hearing the music lifts your spirits and gives
you energy, and you feel like dancing. Your
body moves easily, and you are pain-free.
In the kitchen, you smell freshly baked
cookies. Homemade cookies.
You walk toward the granite countertop
and help yourself to a cookie.
It is still warm, and you can feel the
temperature and texture on your fingers.
Celebrating this experience, you take a bite
of the delightful cookie. It's delicious!
With more energy and joy, you return to the living room.
Your body feels light and easy, and you are free of pain.

You are standing in front of the window, watching

the children playing in the garden.

You take a few deep breaths, appreciating every moment.

Then you sit back down in your favorite chair.

SWIMMING AND FLOATING
ON THE WATER

Find a comfortable place where you are undisturbed.

Depending on your mobility, sit or lie down. Take a deep

breath and hold it for four seconds. Slowly exhale for seven.

Repeat this three times. Enjoy your calm breathing.

Imagine that a cleansing light enters your

body from the crown of your head.

This vibrant light flows through your body, drawing

away all worries, all pain, all tears, all fears—

sweeping healing comfort and fresh energy into your

body. You feel at peace, supported, not alone.

Imagine this abundant healing light coming in and flowing

through to the tips of your fingers, to the tips of your toes,

cleansing and revitalizing every precious part of you.

The light leaves your body, drawing with it all

impurities, leaving you free of disease and anything

that may hinder your happiness and your healing.

Water holds many memories for us, perhaps of sand between our toes, braving the sea with its chill biting our skin, or of jumping high into a blue lagoon from a boat, or of jumping high into a swimming pool. Select your favorite place; it may be in the sea, on the beach, in a pool, where you swam, where you enjoyed the water. Hold tight to that picture.

The day is warm, and the temperature of the water is just right. You are relaxed and grateful to be right where you are. What a beautiful day!

Looking at the water, what can you see? Is a light breeze blowing ripples across the water, or are waves moving powerfully? The sound of water and waves is calming, nurturing in their rhythm and bringing you peace. Your toes are getting wet as you near the water's edge, the waves splashing at your feet. The air warms your face, and you are grateful for the magnificent sun rising just for you each day.

You walk deeper into the water until you become accustomed to the temperature, and then you begin to swim. You exhale a sigh, feeling content. You are weightless and free and relishing each movement.

Floating, lying on top of the water, listening only to the sounds of the water, being taken a little left, a little right, you are drawn by the current. This feeling of your body being so free of limitations, without pain, is truly magical. You float, letting let the water hold you in the palm of its hand. You are small against the nature of the water, feeling supported in your weightlessness, loving this time, knowing you are safe. The water is salty, nourishing your skin, full of healing for you. The salt smell hangs suspended in the air. You are stretching and swimming with bold strokes, going forward. You feel light and empowered, free of restriction, enjoying the abundant freedom and ease of movement. You are energized and relaxed, happy for the gift of water.

HORSEBACK RIDING

· ·

Find a comfortable place where you are undisturbed.

Depending on your mobility, sit or lie down. Take a deep

breath and hold it for four seconds. Slowly exhale for seven.

Repeat this three times. Enjoy your calm breathing.

Imagine that a cleansing light enters your

body from the crown of your head.

This vibrant light flows through your body, drawing

away all worries, all pain, all tears, all fears—

sweeping healing comfort and fresh energy into your

body. You feel at peace, supported, not alone.

Imagine this abundant healing light coming in and flowing

through to the tips of your fingers, to the tips of your toes,

cleansing and revitalizing every precious part of you.

The light leaves your body, drawing with it all

impurities, leaving you free of disease and anything

that may hinder your happiness and your healing.

Remember a time you were astride your horse.
Find yourself; are you in the dressage
arena or outside on a trail?
Your horse is excited to have you back in the saddle, to
be with you, out in the open spaces, in the woodland.
You stride across the grounds, through fields and forest,
enjoying the colors and aroma of flowers and nature. You
feel invigorated by the scenic glory of the countryside.
Riding through the woods, across fields, or in the
arena, you may be accompanied by other riders.
You love the sound of the hooves, almost musical,
moving to a beat, the feel and smell of the leather
saddle, the horse guided by you, moving powerfully,
walking, trotting, then building to a canter.
The horse's mane is flying as you ride. You see the
silky shine of your horse's coat, its breath marking
the air, your hand touching your horse's neck—this
beautiful animal that is so responsive to your touch,
such a dear and loyal friend. You trot with your horse;
you rise and fall in your saddle, set free from worry
and discomfort. Free from any pain and limitations.

In this moment, you are moving easily with
your horse and enjoying every moment.
It is magnificent!

MUSIC AND DANCING

Find a comfortable place where you are undisturbed.

Depending on your mobility sit or lie down. Take a deep

breath and hold it for four seconds. Slowly exhale for seven.

Repeat this three times. Enjoy your calm breathing.

Imagine that a cleansing light enters your

body from the crown of your head.

This vibrant light flows through your body, drawing

away all worries, all pain, all tears, all fears—

sweeping healing comfort and fresh energy into your

body. You feel at peace, supported, not alone.

Imagine this abundant healing light coming in and flowing

through to the tips of your fingers, to the tips of your toes,

cleansing and revitalizing every precious part of you.

The light leaves your body, drawing with it all

impurities, leaving you free of disease and anything

that may hinder your happiness and your healing.

When the music plays, a freedom runs away with the notes, so beautifully and easily put together, nurturing your heart and lifting your spirit. You feel happy.
The music that you are listening to awakens your memories of dancing, of singing, maybe even of whistling and humming.
You may recall being swung around and around as a child.
Or held in an embrace as an adult, swaying and smiling with the pure pleasure that music and dancing brings.
Your feet move effortlessly, feeling the support of the floor.
You are dancing without a care, enjoying the freedom you are feeling. The music fills the room and you move so naturally.
You are aware of the fun of dancing, the freedom and the way your body is feeling.
Energy reaches every part of you. You feel well; you feel exhilarated by the music. You feel invigorated by the exercise; you feel warm in this moment.
You feel the way you always wish to feel.
Continue dancing; enjoy the wonders of movement and music!

"When you dance, your purpose is not to get to a certain place on the floor. It's to enjoy each step along the way."

— Dr. Wayne Dyer

ABOUT THE AUTHORS

Ulrike Berzau, MM, MHS, PT, FACHE, is a certified *Thinking Into Results* consultant with the Proctor Gallagher Institute. She has significant experience as a health care executive, physical therapist, coach, and mentor throughout the United States, the Middle East, and Germany and an impressive track record of leading individuals and organizations to exceptional results. Her list of accomplishments includes the American College of Healthcare Regent's award, Hospital of Choice Top 10, and many other awards. Ulrike is German, has one son, is an avid dressage rider, and lives in the United States.

Christel Cowdrey is a successful entrepreneur and business owner with experience in international research and analysis. She is a linguist, screenwriter and published writer and trained as a presenter in TV and radio. As a natural collaborator and 'student of the mind,' she has followed Jim Rohn, Wayne Dyer, and a host of others for some thirty years and has been mentored by and is a graduate of Bob Proctor's Matrixx. Christel is Swedish, has twin sons and three springer spaniels, sings jazz, is an accomplished cook, and lives in England.

RESOURCES

Behrend, Genevieve. *Your Invisible Power.* Wilder Publication, 2008.

Clarey, Christopher. "Olympians Use Imagery as Mental Training." *New York Times,* February 22, 2014.

Maltz, Dr. Maxwell. *The New Psycho-Cybernetics.* Prentice Hall Press, 2001.

Proctor, Bob. *The Winner's Image.* LifeSuccess Corporate, 1995.

Proctor, Bob, and Sandra Gallagher. *Thinking Into Results.* LifeSuccess Corporate, 2009.

Savoie, Jane. *That Winning Feeling! A New Approach to Riding Using Psychocybernetics.* Trafalgar Square, 1992.

The Cure Is ... Transform Your Health. www.thecureismovie.com, 2012.